MW01680958

# A GUIDE TO EFFECTIVE PRAYER

## Partner with God to Accomplish His Will on the Earth

KADE YOUNG

Copyright © 2026 by Kade Young

All rights reserved. No part of this book may be reproduced in any form by an electronic or mechanical means, including information storage and retrieval systems, without permission in writing from the copyright owner, except by a reviewer who may quote brief passages in a review.

Questions or bulk orders? Contact books@kadeyoung.com

ISBN (Paperback): 978-1-7377322-9-7

Scripture quotations marked NLT are taken from the Holy Bible, New Living Translation, copyright © 1996, 2004, 2015 by Tyndale House Foundation. Used by permission of Tyndale House Publishers, Inc., Carol Stream, Illinois 60188. All rights reserved. Scripture quotations marked NKJV are taken from the New King James Version®. Copyright © 1982 by Thomas Nelson. Used by permission. All rights reserved. Scripture quotations marked AMPC are taken from the Amplified Bible, Copyright © 1954, 1958, 1962, 1964, 1965, 1987 by The Lockman Foundation. Used by Permission.

# Contents

1

# God Wants to Hear You

Timid prayers are ineffective prayers. They get confused with humility, but only expose that we don't know who we are to God.

We don't have to wonder how God wants us to approach Him in prayer, because it's made clear in the scriptures: come boldly.[1]

**When we pray, we must be confident that God wants to hear us.**

We must know, without a doubt, that it is our blood-bought right to ask God for anything we need—fully expecting that He will give it to us.

Jesus demonstrated this for us in His final prayer before the cross (recorded in John 17). There was no trace of timidly or reserve in His prayer. He knew who He was to God, and wasn't afraid to remind Him of it.

His requests were bold. He didn't wonder if God would do it. He knew God would do it. So it actually sounded more like demanding than asking.

However, Jesus was not acting like a spoiled brat. He was revealing to us what it sounds like to be a confident Son who knows His Father.

How do we know we should approach God the same way?

> **Romans 8:15-17 NLT** – So you have not received a spirit that makes you fearful slaves. Instead, you received God's Spirit when he adopted you as his own children. Now we call him, "Abba, Father." For his Spirit joins with our spirit to affirm that we are God's children. And since we are his children, we are his heirs. In fact, together with Christ we are heirs of God's glory. But if we are to share his glory, we must also share his suffering.

If this is hard for you to grasp, all you need to do is follow the example of Jesus. Start your prayers with a reminder of who you are to God, like this:

"Father, Your blood-bought son (daughter) is here. Now that I'm in Christ, I belong to You, and You belong to me. I know you want to hear me. You promised that anything I ask in Jesus' name, You'll do. And I believe it because I know You are a good Father who gives good gifts to His children..."

Starting your prayer like this will leave no room for timid, pitiful prayers.

From this point forward, every time you pray, pray like God wants to hear you. Because He does.

2

# God Wants to Speak to You

Prayer was never meant to be a one-sided conversation. God has something to say every time you pray.

> **John 16:13-14 NLT** – When the Spirit of truth comes, he will guide you into all truth. He will not speak on his own but will tell you what he has heard. He will tell you about the future. He will bring me glory by telling you whatever he receives from me.

The Holy Spirit is continually speaking to us in perfect alignment with Jesus. He reminds us of what Jesus said. He teaches us the things Jesus wasn't able to when He was on the earth. He even tells us what's to come.

If you think that only church leaders or prophets can hear from God, you've believed a lie.

Jesus didn't put stipulations around hearing the Holy Spirit. What He said in John 16 applies to all of His followers. Every. Single. One.

Which begs the question, why do so many Christians say they've never heard the voice of God?

Because they haven't learned to listen.

Have you ever talked to someone who wasn't listening? Their ears heard what you said, but their mind was distracted. They weren't really listening.

This is what we do to the Holy Spirit. We allow ourselves to get distracted by worry, fear, disappointment... Our minds are so occupied with the things we've been redeemed from that we aren't able to listen to what the Holy Spirit is saying.

Only when we choose to quiet our minds by taking every thought captive[1] are we able to hear the voice of the Holy Spirit.

Now's the time to stop blaming your lack of listening on the Holy Spirit. Repent for accusing Him of not speaking to you.

Then, develop the skill of quieting your mind so you can listen and obey.

He has the answer to every problem. Instead of worrying, ask the Holy Spirit what to do and trust what He reveals.

If you don't hear Him immediately, it's not because He is withholding. It's because you are still preoccupied in your mind. Take time to quiet your mind and ask again.

Believe that God wants to speak to you. Not because I said it, but because Jesus already told you He would.

3

# Pray Like Jesus

Religious leaders have always been considered the experts in prayer. But, Jesus is not impressed with professional prayers like we are.

Thankfully, the disciples asked Him how to pray, and His response is recorded in the scriptures:

> **Matthew 6:9-13 NKJV** – In this manner, therefore, pray: Our Father in heaven, Hallowed be Your name. Your kingdom come. Your will be done On earth as it is in heaven. Give us this day our daily bread. And forgive us our debts, As we forgive our debtors. And do not lead us into temptation, But deliver us from the evil one. For Yours is the kingdom and the power and the glory forever. Amen.

Everything we need to know about prayer is revealed in this short example from Jesus.

**Our Father...**

Notice He didn't say "My Father." What a joy this brings! We have been adopted into the family of God; we are co-heirs with Christ![1]

That's why we must begin each prayer with full confidence that we belong in the presence of our Father. We are not addressing a distant God. We are boldly entering the presence of our Heavenly Father.

But there's even more we can learn from these opening two words. Our prayers should never be self-focused. It's not "MY Father"; it's "OUR Father."

We should always approach God with the Body of Christ in mind. After all, we are all one in Christ.

**...in heaven, hallowed be Your name.**

Lest we get too casual with our Heavenly Father, we must always remember that He is above it all.

Many things are fighting for first place in our lives. That's why, every time we pray, we must intentionally look up and keep God in that place.

Knowing God as "Father" must always be paired with the fear of the Lord. Love and reverence complete each other.

**Your kingdom come.**

We are promised that if our focus is on His kingdom, all of our earthly needs will be met.[2] But how easy it is to get distracted by the things of this life.

That's why we must always re-align our focus in prayer every day, keeping our eyes on His kingdom.

**YOUR WILL BE DONE ON EARTH AS IT IS IN HEAVEN.**

It does not please God when we pray, "If it be Your will..." because He already revealed His will to us through Jesus Christ.[3]

Therefore, we must cooperate with what we already know He wants to do on the earth. We must agree with it and call it forth in prayer.

His will is guaranteed in Heaven. But on the earth, it requires our partnership. Not because He can't override us, but because He won't.

God gave dominion over the earth to us[4], so we must partner with Him in prayer by boldly declaring His will to be done.

**GIVE US THIS DAY OUR DAILY BREAD.**

We must approach our Father with full confidence that He will give us not only the physical resources we need for the day, but the spiritual resources.

We are not to worry about tomorrow or try to survive off of what we got yesterday. Our expectation should be a daily encounter with the presence and provision of God.

And notice the word "us." Another reminder not to get self-focused in prayer. Make it about our needs being met, not just yours.

Don't let a day go by that you don't reach out and unapologetically receive His provision for that day.

**Forgive us our debts, as we forgive our debtors.**

The forgiveness that comes from God through Jesus Christ is too great to hold onto. It comes in such abundance that is must overflow.

If you struggle to give forgiveness it's because you have yet to receive forgiveness.

And clearly, this isn't something you do one time and call it good. In every prayer, we must revel in God's forgiveness. He is full of mercy!

Putting ourselves in constant remembrance of His abundance of forgiveness towards us produces a flow of unending forgiveness towards others. Oh, how we need this every day!

**Do not lead us into temptation, but deliver us from the evil one.**

The scriptures say that God does not tempt us to do evil.[5] And for every temptation, He provides a way out.[6]

This confirms that, although temptation comes, it is not from God. Our great enemy, the devil, is prowling around, looking for someone to devour.

Only God can expose the deception and deliver us from every trap.

We don't go to Him whining about the temptation. We go to Him for the answer, because we know He has it and wants us to have it.

**For Yours is the kingdom and the power and the glory forever.**

David demonstrated this for us in the Psalms. Yes, we can take our problems to God. But we must always end our prayer by remembering how great God is.

Since we are in His kingdom, we have nothing to worry about. Since all power belongs to Him, our enemies do not intimidate us.

Since the glory belongs to Him, we know He will dish out His goodness liberally and frequently on all who believe.

**Pray like Jesus.**

This is how Jesus taught us to pray. Nice and simple. Don't make it more complicated than it needs to be.

You may have realized that you need to correct your approach to God. Here's the good news: You can do that now.

No more pitiful "if it be thy will" prayers. Go to Him boldly every day. In His presence, you'll find everything you need and more.

# 4

# Pray in the Spirit

Praying in the spirit, also known as speaking in tongues, is one of the most divisive subjects in the church. Entire denominations are formed based on this one thing alone!

Any time division enters the church, we know the enemy is at work. Instead of yielding to the temptation to fight with each other, we should dive in and find out why the enemy is so threatened by these subjects.

According to the Bible, speaking in tongues is a gift given through the Holy Spirit for the age we live in.[1]

They didn't have it before the day of Pentecost, and it will no longer be needed in the age to come. It is only for right now.

Although speaking in tongues is not a requirement for salvation, all who are saved should earnestly desire this ability through the Holy Spirit. After all, we are told to pray in the spirit at all times and on every occasion.[2] It sure would be hard to fulfill that command if you can't do it to begin with.

To illustrate the importance of praying in the spirit, I want to share a prophetic word that came to NoLimits Church on March 31, 2025.

**Prophetic Word**

*Remember that when you pray in the spirit, you pray forth mysteries.*[3] *You are praying for things you don't know what to pray.*

*When you pray in the spirit, you are praying forth the perfect plan of God, and it is coming to pass as you pray it out because no word that comes from the Spirit returns to Him void.*[4]

*As you pray in the spirit, it is a great gift that I've given you for these last days, says the Lord.*

*You need to pray in the spirit so you can make your way in the path that I've called you to. As you pray in the spirit, you are lighting up the path, says the Lord.*

*Your mind tells you that you are not getting anything done, but your mind is lying to you. For My Word declares that when you pray in the spirit, you are praying out My plan.*[5] *You are praying forth My words and My words do not return to Me void.*

*Therefore, pray in the spirit with great boldness and confidence knowing that as you do, things are happening in the spirit that will also happen on the earth.*

*Pray, pray, pray in the spirit without ceasing! For it is a weapon I have given you, says the Lord, to defeat the enemy. When you pray in the spirit, the enemy doesn't even know what's coming at him. Your enemy gets destroyed as you pray in the spirit.*

### How to Respond

If you already have the ability to speak in tongues, this is your prod to do it more often.

You'll be tempted to belittle it and shy away from it. Let all those temptations fuel you to pray in the spirit even more.

If you don't have the ability, don't sweat it. Stir up your confidence that God wants you to have it, and keep asking until you get it. Pray this:

"Father, Your word says that You give the Holy Spirit to those who keep asking for it.[6] With confidence, here I am, once again, asking You for what You promised. I want to pray in tongues, and I know that You want me to as well. Reveal any doubt getting in the way. Fill me now so I can pray Your perfect plan through the Spirit!"

# 5

# Partner with God

It's only by speaking in alignment with God that His will is done on the earth.

If we refuse to speak, then things can't happen. But if we multiply our speaking, we'll see a multiplication of God's will in the earth.

There's a lot that has to get done for us to see what we want to see. That's why we must be persistent in our prayers. We are speaking out the plan of God!

He knows exactly what to do. As we pray in the spirit, we pray out those plans one step at a time. But we must keep praying so the work can keep moving forward.

Think of the complexity of what God has to do to accomplish His will on the earth. He has to infiltrate every area of society.

We have the privilege of giving Him access, through our words, to accomplish His plan in our families, cities, churches, and around the world.

But it only happens as we pray. If we refuse to pray, these things will not get done.

What we perceive as a lack of God moving is directly attached to our lack of praying.

This is a partnership. And we need to be more aware of our part in the partnership.

God brings the power, authority, and glory. We simply give Him access to accomplish His will through our prayers.

Let this reframe the way you approach prayer. You are not trying to convince God to do something. **You are partnering with God so He can do what He's always wanted to do.**

# About the Author

## KADE YOUNG

**Kade Young** is on mission to help believers move from a place of working FOR Jesus to working WITH Him.

As an apostle of Jesus Christ, he writes quick, hard-hitting reads that ignite boldness, activate miracles, and reveal what it truly means to walk in the Spirit.

He leads NoLimits Church, equipping believers to walk in supernatural authority, and founded Collaborate Worship, helping churches worldwide create incredible sound for powerful worship.

Beyond ministry, Kade is a husband, a father of six, and a newbie farmer on a wild adventure raising sheep, cattle, and chickens with his family.

Learn more at **kadeyoung.com**

MORE BOOKS BY

# KADE YOUNG

## 7 Spirits of God
Unlock the Fullness
of the Holy Spirit

ORDER BOOKS ON AMAZON

## Love Hijacked
Return to Your First Love
Before It's Too Late

## Jesus Ain't Woke
Your Wake-Up Call to
Stop Tolerating Sin

## God's End-Time Wealth Transfer
Position Yourself for Great Wealth
to Fund the End-Time Harvest

## Ancient Roots of the LGBTQ Movement
Exposing the Demonic War on
Gender, Sexuality, and Biblical Truth

# Endnotes

God Wants to Hear You

1. Hebrews 4:16

God Wants to Speak to You

1. 2 Corinthians 10:5

Pray Like Jesus

1. Romans 8:17
2. Matthew 6:33
3. John 6:38
4. Genesis 1:26
5. James 1:13
6. 1 Corinthians 10:13

Pray in the Spirit

1. Mark 16:17
2. Ephesians 6:18
3. 1 Corinthians 14:2
4. Isaiah 55:11
5. 1 Corinthians 14:2
6. Luke 11:13

Made in the USA
Coppell, TX
07 March 2026

73190296R00017